NATIONAL
GEOGRAPHIC
KiDS

weird
but
true!

CHRISTMAS

300 festive facts
to light up the holidays

NATIONAL GEOGRAPHIC KiDS

weird but true!

CHRISTMAS

300 festive facts to light up the holidays

NATIONAL GEOGRAPHIC
WASHINGTON, D.C.

IT'S NOT JUST A **WINTER MYTH!**

YOUR TONGUE REALLY CAN GET **STUCK** TO A PIECE OF FROZEN METAL.

Don't try this at home!

A Canadian scientist **built a** machine that grows icicles.

A business magazine once listed **SANTA** as one of the **WORLD'S RICHEST PEOPLE.**

THE WORLD'S BIGGEST CHRISTMAS BAUBLE ORNAMENT IS WIDER THAN A GARAGE DOOR AND AS HEAVY AS A BUFFALO.

THE PINE NEEDLES ON SOME CHRISTMAS TREES ARE EDIBLE.

Do not eat any leaves without an adult's guidance.

The world's **longest** CHRISTMAS LIST stretched **13,053** feet (3,979 m) and took **1 hour** and **40 minutes** to be unrolled.

THE BERRIES OF SOME MISTLETOE PLANTS EXPLODE.

"The Christmas Song (CHESTNUTS ROASTING ON AN OPEN FIRE)" was written during a summer heat wave.

YOU ARE MORE LIKELY TO FIND ICICLES HANGING ON THE SOUTH SIDE OF A BUILDING THAN THE NORTH SIDE.

Donner and **Blitzen** were originally called **Dunder** and **Blixem.**

PEOPLE IN PARTS OF SOUTH AFRICA SNACK ON **DEEP-FRIED CATERPILLARS** ON CHRISTMAS DAY.

There is EGGNOG-flavored lip balm.

IN INDIA, PEOPLE DECORATE BANANA TREES FOR CHRISTMAS.

OF ADULT REINDEER, ONLY FEMALES KEEP THEIR ANTLERS THROUGH DECEMBER. (THAT MEANS SANTA'S REINDEER ARE PROBABLY ALL GIRLS!)

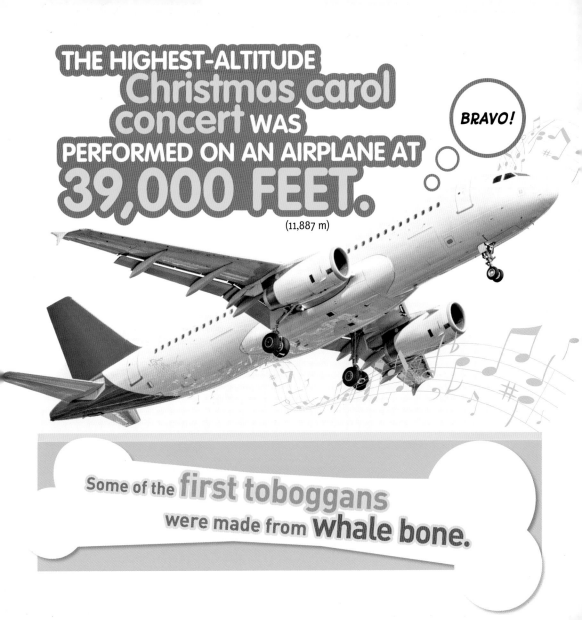

THE HIGHEST-ALTITUDE **Christmas carol concert** WAS PERFORMED ON AN AIRPLANE AT **39,000 FEET.**

(11,887 m)

BRAVO!

Some of the **first toboggans** were made from **whale bone.**

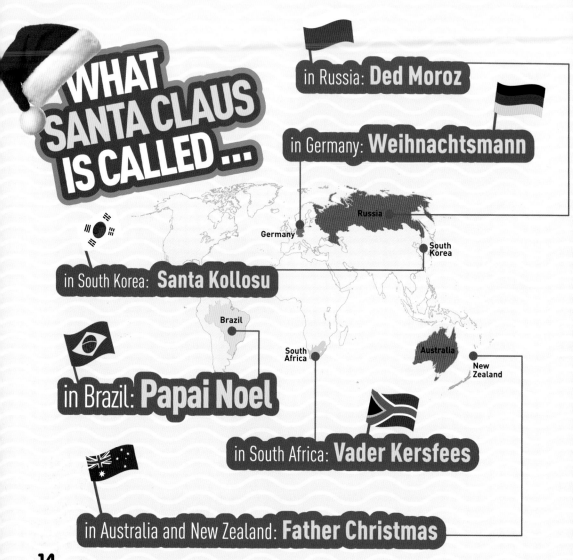

WHAT SANTA CLAUS IS CALLED ...

in Russia: **Ded Moroz**

in Germany: **Weihnachtsmann**

in South Korea: **Santa Kollosu**

in Brazil: **Papai Noel**

in South Africa: **Vader Kersfees**

in Australia and New Zealand: **Father Christmas**

Germany

Russia

South Korea

Brazil

South Africa

Australia

New Zealand

98 percent of **Christmas trees** are **grown** on **farms.**

Italian children look out for **Befana**, a friendly witch who comes down the chimney to bring candy and toys on Christmas.

Sugarplums DO NOT CONTAIN PLUMS— they're SEEDS or NUTS dipped in SUGAR.

EVERY SNOWFLAKE HAS SIX SIDES.

AN OFFICIAL GOVERNMENT WEBSITE TRACKS **THE MOVEMENT** of **SANTA'S SLEIGH ON CHRISTMAS EVE.**

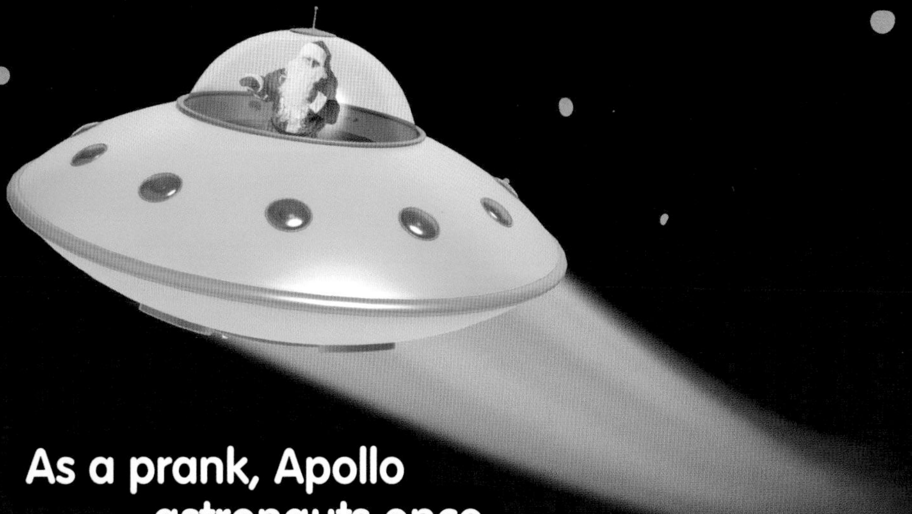

As a prank, Apollo astronauts once **radioed NASA** that they had seen a **UFO piloted** by someone in **A RED SUIT.**

FAR OUT!

Branches *of* icicles are called legs.

Old Christmas trees can be used to rebuild sand dunes after a hurricane.

On January 10, 1915, snowflakes measuring **four inches** (10 cm) fell across Berlin, Germany.

This snowflake is **FOUR INCHES.**

INCHES

1
2
3
4

INCHES

1
2
3
4

22

MYSTERY ELVES HAVE BEEN SPOTTED IN DETROIT, MICHIGAN, U.S.A., PASSING OUT $100 BILLS TO STRANGERS.

The snowflake moray eel has two jaws to help it snatch its prey.

You can buy **pickle-, gravy-, and bacon-flavored candy canes.**

THE UNITED STATES GROWS **MORE THAN**

Cook County, Illinois, U.S.A., uses old Christmas trees to build habitats for wild animals.

ASPIRING MALL SANTAS CAN LEARN THE JOB AT THE INTERNATIONAL UNIVERSITY OF **SANTA CLAUS.**

40 MILLION POINSETTIAS EVERY YEAR.

U.S. PRESIDENT THEODORE ROOSEVELT BANNED CHRISTMAS TREES FROM THE WHITE HOUSE.

Good King Wenceslas was a real ruler in medieval Bohemia.

Candy canes started off as straight white sticks.

Some scholars think that *Jesus* may have actually been born *in the* spring.

An American woman set the **record** for the most **Christmas trees** chopped down in two minutes: **27.**

AN **18-MILE** (29-KM) **FROZEN STRETCH** IN BRITISH COLUMBIA, CANADA, IS THE **LONGEST ICE-SKATING** TRAIL ON EARTH.

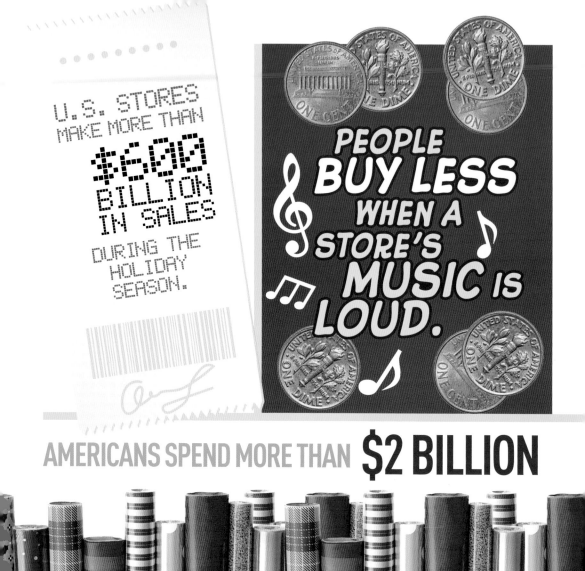

U.S. STORES MAKE MORE THAN **$600 BILLION IN SALES** DURING THE HOLIDAY SEASON.

PEOPLE **BUY LESS** WHEN A STORE'S **MUSIC** IS **LOUD.**

AMERICANS SPEND MORE THAN **$2 BILLION**

A **170-year-old** *hand-colored Christmas card once sold at auction for nearly* **$30,000.**

A YEAR ON WRAPPING PAPER.

33

SNOW SOMETIMES APPEARS BLUE.

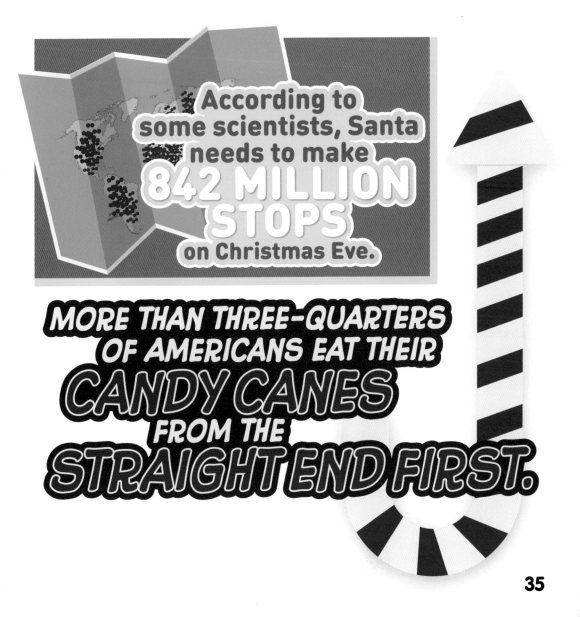

According to some scientists, Santa needs to make **842 MILLION STOPS** on Christmas Eve.

MORE THAN THREE-QUARTERS OF AMERICANS EAT THEIR CANDY CANES FROM THE STRAIGHT END FIRST.

IN 1853, **FRANKLIN PIERCE** BECAME THE FIRST U.S. PRESIDENT TO HAVE A **CHRISTMAS TREE** AT THE **WHITE HOUSE.**

On Christmas Eve in Norway, some families hide their **brooms** so that **evil witches** won't steal them **overnight.**

TELLING GHOST STORIES *was a Christmas tradition in Victorian-era England.*

The famous Christmas song "Let It Snow!" never mentions Christmas.

Before the invention of electric **Christmas lights,** people put **lit candles** on their **trees.**

Each Christmas, a building in California, U.S.A., is topped with a red bow that's as wide as a tennis court.

THERE ARE **1,300** SPECIES OF MISTLETOE.

38

IN BRAZIL, FAMILIES DECORATE PINE TREES WITH LITTLE PIECES OF COTTON TO REPRESENT FALLING SNOW.

The average person spends a total of

19 hours CHRISTMAS SHOPPING EACH YEAR.

IF YOU WERE FLYING SANTA'S SLEIGH, YOU'D HAVE TO TRAVEL 1,280 MILES (2,060 km/s) PER SECOND TO REACH EVERYONE IN TIME.

THE WORLD'S LARGEST GINGERBREAD HOUSE WAS A TWO-STORY HOME.

IT WAS MADE WITH:

1,800 pounds (816 kg) of **butter**

7,200 **eggs**

3,000 pounds (1,361 kg) of **sugar**

22,000 pieces of **candy**

World's Larges

Ingredients

41

SCIENTISTS AT THE **NORTH POLE** WORK ON **FLOATING** RESEARCH STATIONS.

THAT'S WEIRD!

Factories in Shijiao, China, recycle discarded Christmas lights into slipper soles.

"JINGLE BELLS" WAS THE FIRST CHRISTMAS CAROL PLAYED IN SPACE.

THERE IS A
HIP-HOP VERSION
OF THE BALLET
THE NUTCRACKER.

THE 12 DAYS OF CHRISTMAS ACTUALLY **COME AFTER** CHRISTMAS.

In medieval times, holiday revelers *feasted* on stuffed *peacocks* and *boar meat.*

A Canadian man has a collection of more than **25,000** items featuring Santa Claus.

45

THERE ARE TOWNS IN THE UNITED STATES CALLED ...

Eggnog

Silver Bell

North Pole

Jolly

UTAH

UNITED

ARIZONA

TEXAS

ALASKA

STATES

MICHIGAN

KENTUCKY

GEORGIA

Christmas

Mistletoe

Santa Claus

A LAYER OF FRESH SNOW ABSORBS SOUND WAVES.

A HOTEL IN DUBAI, UNITED ARAB EMIRATES, **DISPLAYED**

A CHRISTMAS TREE COVERED IN

181 PIECES OF JEWELRY

VALUED AT MORE THAN **$11 MILLION.**

People in the United Kingdom traditionally **bake coins, buttons, thimbles,** *or* **wishbones** *into Christmas desserts.*

Early **SLEDS** were discovered on an excavated **VIKING SHIP.**

50

THE WORLD'S LARGEST
**CHRISTMAS
PUDDING**
WEIGHED MORE THAN
A HIPPO.

IN BRITAIN, EATING A **MINCE PIE** FOR EACH OF THE **12 DAYS** OF **CHRISTMAS** IS SAID TO BRING **G**✸✸**D LUCK.**

Some scientists are trying to clone evergreens to create the perfect Christmas tree.

Some stores hire psychologists to help them predict what gifts shoppers are most likely to buy.

1,762 =

PARTICIPANTS IN THE WORLD'S LARGEST
GATHERING OF PEOPLE
DRESSED LIKE CHRISTMAS ELVES

56

The star of **Bethlehem** (SAID TO HAVE BEEN SEEN DURING JESUS' BIRTH) may have been a **supernova.**

The earliest Christmas trees—dating back to 1510—were decorated with apples and paper roses.

Visitors to a museum in Virginia, U.S.A., can perform **experiments** on **holiday fruitcake.**

Tinsel **was** **once made out of thin pieces of** **real silver.**

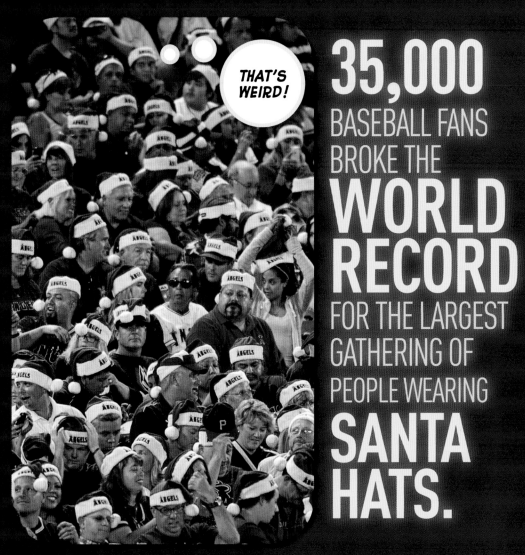

THAT'S WEIRD!

35,000
BASEBALL FANS BROKE THE
WORLD RECORD
FOR THE LARGEST GATHERING OF PEOPLE WEARING
SANTA HATS.

Reindeer
hooves
expand in the
summer and **shrink**
in the winter.

A reindeer's
antlers
WEIGH MORE than a
car tire.

Some reindeer **herds** have as many as **500,000** reindeer.

Reindeer **hairs** are **hollow.**

61

Kids in Iceland fear **the Yule Cat,** a mythical monster who is said to eat children at Christmastime.

IN THE **1960s,** SOME CHRISTMAS TREES WERE MADE OF THE SAME **METAL** AS **SODA CANS.**

$500 $500

Today, collectors pay up to $500 for the rare trees.

$500 $500

A **SINGLE SNOW-STORM** CAN DROP

40 MILLION TONS
(36.3 million t)

OF SNOW.

Rudolph the Red-Nosed Reindeer was almost named Reginald.

364 = the total number of gifts given in the song "The Twelve Days of Christmas"

In Caracas, Venezuela, it's tradition to **roller-skate to church** on Christmas Day.

Mathematicians study how fast checkout lines move when people are Christmas shopping.

IS IT HOT IN HERE?

AT AN ANNUAL FESTIVAL IN ZURICH, SWITZERLAND, PEOPLE BLOW UP A GIANT SNOWMAN FILLED WITH FIREWORKS.

ONE OF THE WORLD'S **TALLEST** LIVING CHRISTMAS TREES— A **162-FOOT** [49-m] FIR IN IDAHO, U.S.A. IS DECORATED WITH MORE THAN **TWO MILES** [3.2 km] OF LIGHTS EACH YEAR.

SOME POINSETTIA PLANTS CAN GROW TALLER THAN A BASKETBALL HOOP.

PEOPLE USED TO **DECORATE** THEIR CHRISTMAS TREES WITH **BOXES OF ANIMAL CRACKERS.**

FRIED CHICKEN IS THE MOST POPULAR CHRISTMAS EVE MEAL IN JAPAN.

National Candy Cane Day is celebrated on December 26 in the United States.

The 1946 Christmas classic *It's a Wonderful Life* used a combination of soap and a fire-fighting chemical to make fake movie snow.

"Snow" was once made on movie sets by painting cornflakes white.

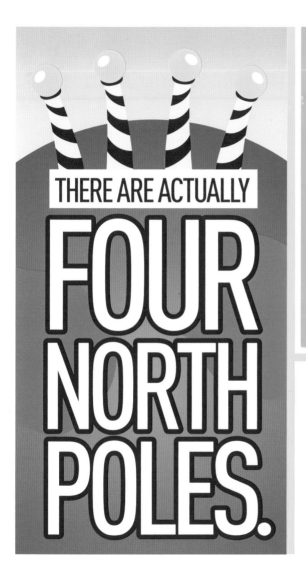

THERE ARE ACTUALLY

FOUR NORTH POLES.

Christmas caroling began as *"wassailing,"* an Old English custom of *greeting* and *toasting friends.*

U.S. president Andrew Jackson once held an **indoor** snowball fight at the **White House.**

74

The fastest time for a marathoner in **A GINGERBREAD MAN** costume is **3 HOURS 29 MINUTES.**

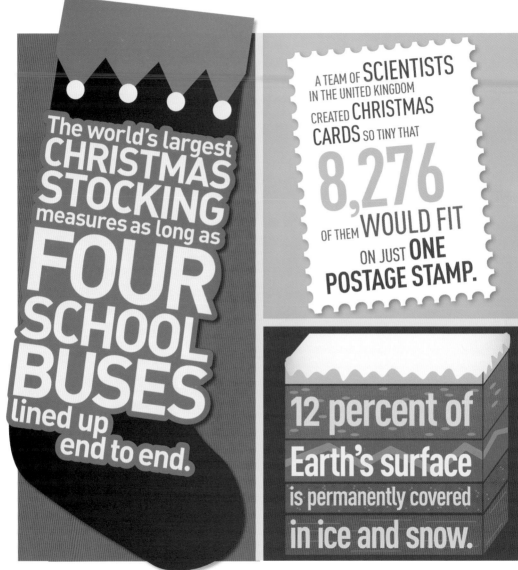

The world's largest CHRISTMAS STOCKING measures as long as FOUR SCHOOL BUSES lined up end to end.

A TEAM OF SCIENTISTS IN THE UNITED KINGDOM CREATED CHRISTMAS CARDS SO TINY THAT 8,276 OF THEM WOULD FIT ON JUST ONE POSTAGE STAMP.

12 percent of Earth's surface is permanently covered in ice and snow.

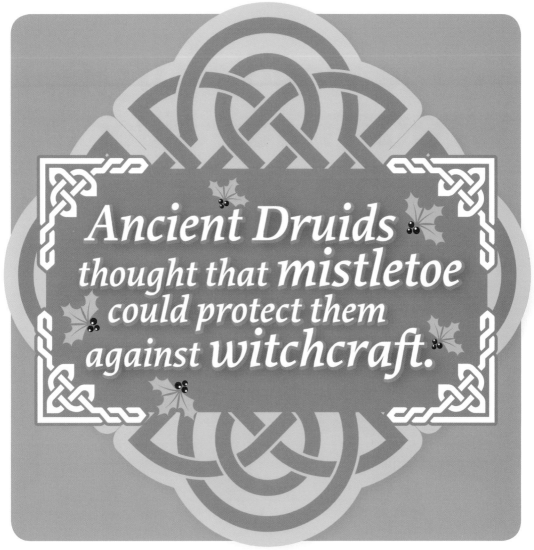

Ancient Druids thought that **mistletoe** could protect them against **witchcraft.**

The world's **largest wreath** was wider than a soccer field and heavier than **two elephants.**

IN UKRAINE, PEOPLE **DECORATE** THEIR CHRISTMAS TREES WITH **FAKE SPIDERS**  **AND WEBS.**

THE LARGEST CUP OF HOT CHOCOLATE EVER MADE COULD HAVE FILLED 20 BATHTUBS.

TUDOR CHRISTMAS PIE =
- a pigeon **inside**
- a partridge **inside**
- a chicken **inside**
- a goose **inside**
- a turkey **inside**
- a pie **crust**

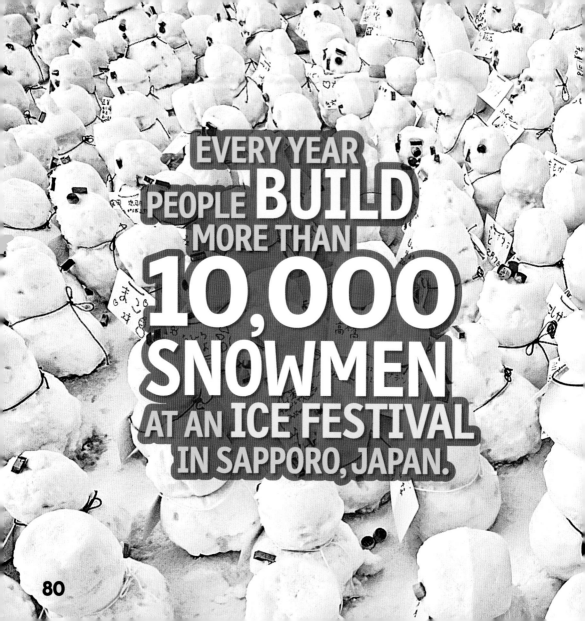

EVERY YEAR PEOPLE **BUILD** MORE THAN **10,000 SNOWMEN** AT AN **ICE FESTIVAL** IN SAPPORO, JAPAN.

One snowflake can contain **180 billion** molecules of water.

QUEEN ELIZABETH I had a baker create LIFE-SIZE *GINGERBREAD COOKIE MODELS of her important* ROYAL GUESTS.

THE LARGEST GATHERING OF PEOPLE WEARING HOLIDAY-THEMED SWEATERS: 3,473 PEOPLE, AT A BASKETBALL GAME IN KANSAS, U.S.A.

IN FLORIDA, U.S.A., PEOPLE MAKE SNOWMEN OUT OF SAND.

WHAT KIDS AROUND THE WORLD LEAVE OUT FOR SANTA

UNITED KINGDOM: MINCE PIES

FRANCE: BISCUITS

SWEDEN: COFFEE

CHILE: SPONGE CAKE

DENMARK: RICE PUDDING

UNITED STATES: COOKIES AND MILK

The state song of Maryland, U.S.A., is sung to the tune of "O Christmas Tree."

PEOPLE IN CANADA BUILT **A GIANT SNOW MAZE** THAT'S NEARLY THE SIZE OF **FOUR** PROFESSIONAL BASKETBALL COURTS PUT TOGETHER.

88

89

A man legally named **Santa Claus** was elected to the city council of North Pole, Alaska, U.S.A., in 2015.

WHITE LIGHTNING

=

A THUNDERSTORM
WHILE IT'S SNOWING

THE TOWN GÄVLE, SWEDEN, **ERECTS A GIANT STRAW GOAT AT CHRISTMAS.**

THE YULE GOAT HAS ITS

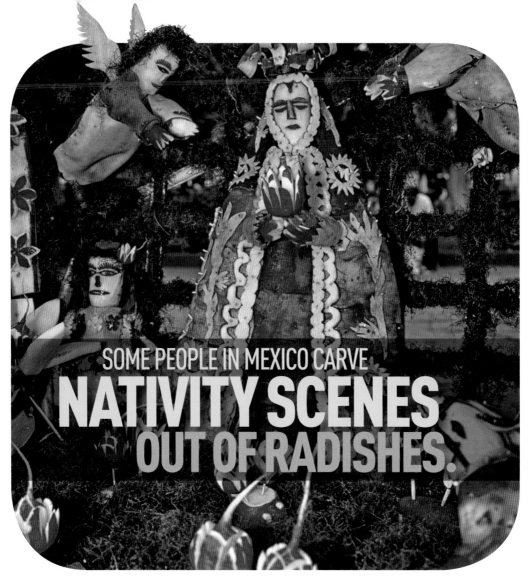

SOME PEOPLE IN MEXICO CARVE
NATIVITY SCENES
OUT OF RADISHES.

700,000,000

According to one calculation, **Santa's sleigh weighs around 700 million pounds.**

(317.5 million kg)

CHRISTMAS DINNER ABOARD THE INTERNATIONAL SPACE STATION HAS INCLUDED TURKEY AND POTATOES IN PLASTIC POUCHES.

ASTRONAUTS ON AN AMERICAN SPACE STATION ONCE

MADE A CHRISTMAS TREE OUT OF FOOD CANS.

It takes up to **10 years** to grow a Christmas tree.

EACH YEAR, PEOPLE IN THE UNITED STATES SPEND SOME $1.6 BILLION ON HOLIDAY CANDY.

AMERICANS PREFER chocolate Santas to chocolate snowmen, according to a recent survey.

A whole **sheep's head** is **considered** a holiday delicacy in Norway.

ICE-SKATING MAY HAVE BEEN **INVENTED** 5,000 **YEARS AGO IN FINLAND.**

THE MAN WHO WROTE "ROCKIN' AROUND THE CHRISTMAS TREE" DIDN'T CELEBRATE CHRISTMAS.

CHARACTERS FROM STAR WARS

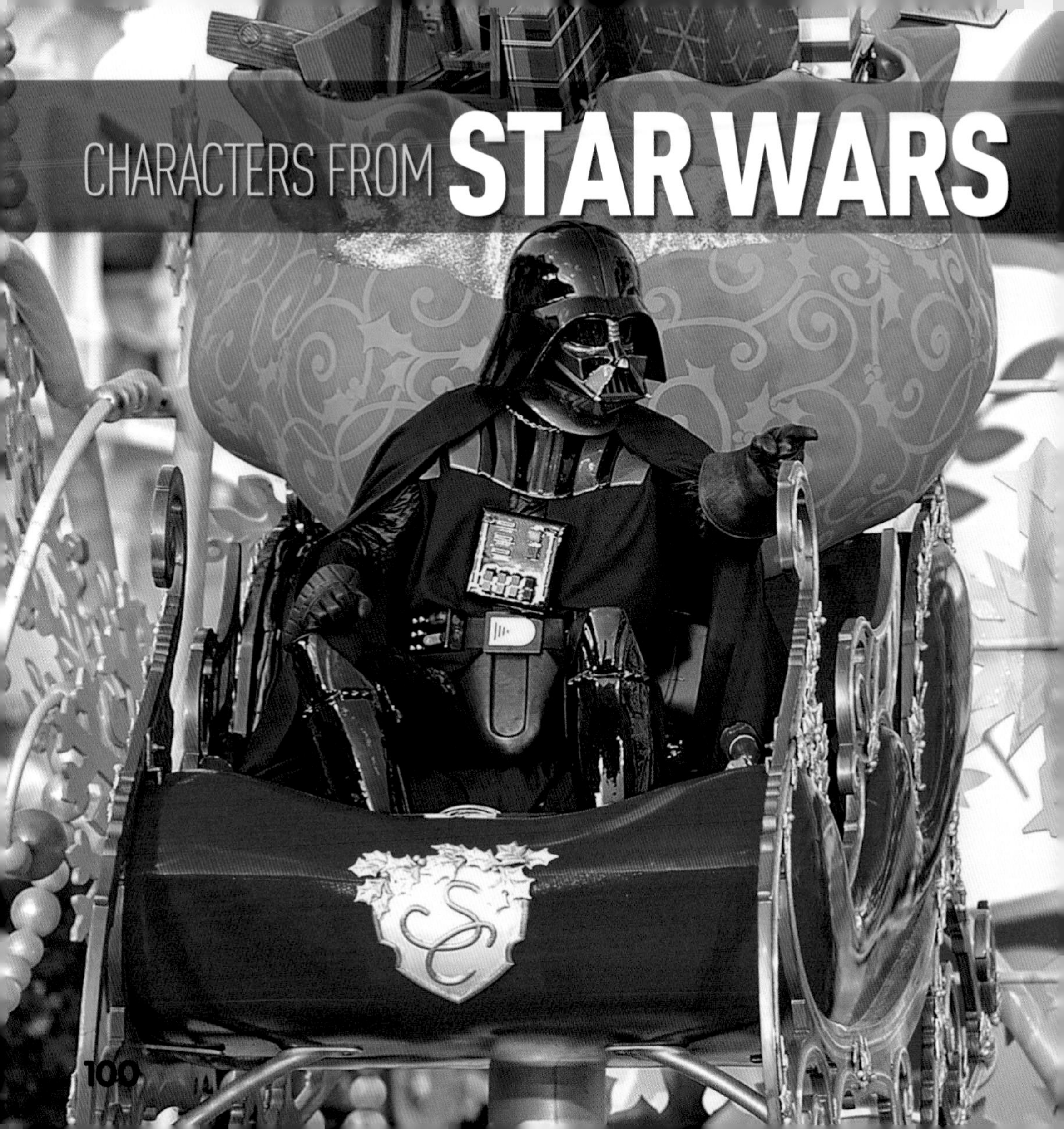

RECORDED A **CHRISTMAS ALBUM.**

SONGS INCLUDE "R2-D2 WE WISH YOU A MERRY CHRISTMAS" AND "WHAT CAN YOU GET A WOOKIEE FOR CHRISTMAS (WHEN HE ALREADY OWNS A COMB?)."

In parts of England, people celebrate Christmas by jumping in icy water.

In Finland, you can study to be Santa's helper at the Elf Training Academy.

A team in India once constructed **a giant Christmas decoration** as **tall as a 10-story building.**

THE WORLD'S LARGEST CANDY CANE WAS AS LONG AS A GRAY WHALE.

A **mass of sliding snow** can weigh as much as **a million tons.** (907,000 t)

CHRISTMAS TREE WORMS CAN

LIVE FOR MORE THAN **40 YEARS.**

RESIDENTS OF SAN DIEGO, CALIFORNIA, U.S.A., FACE A **$250 FINE** IF THEY KEEP THEIR CHRISTMAS LIGHTS UP PAST FEBRUARY 2.

IN THE UNITED STATES ALONE, PEOPLE SPEND MORE THAN

$1 BILLION

EVERY YEAR ON LIVE CHRISTMAS TREES (AND ANOTHER $1.9 BILLION ON FAKE ONES).

IN FRANCE,
ST. NICHOLAS RIDES A
DONKEY BEARING
TOYS FOR KIDS.

People in Europe once hung their **Christmas trees from the ceiling** to keep them out of the **reach of children.**

Masked "belsnicklers" go from house to house in parts of Canada asking for treats during the holidays.

IN PARTS OF SPAIN, POPULAR CHRISTMAS DECORATIONS OF PEOPLE USING THE BATHROOM SYMBOLIZE GOOD FORTUNE.

People in Ethiopia, Kazakhstan, Egypt, and Serbia celebrate Christmas on January 7.

109

Male snowy owls **get** **whiter** as they get **older.**

A strongman dressed as Santa set a world record by pulling a **17.5-TON** (16-t) **"SLEIGH"** full of **GOODIES** down a street in Ontario, Canada.

During the Australian gold rush, people baked **gold nuggets** into their Christmas pudding for **good luck.**

IN UKRAINE, PEOPLE SCATTER HAY ON THE TABLE AT CHRISTMAS DINNER.

Some of the original British settlers in North America **banned Christmas** *and fined anyone who was found celebrating it.*

IN THE SOUTHERN HEMISPHERE, CHRISTMAS COMES IN THE MIDDLE OF THE SUMMER.

DARTER FISH SPORT RED AND GREEN STRIPES.

Yule Lads = Icelandic Santas

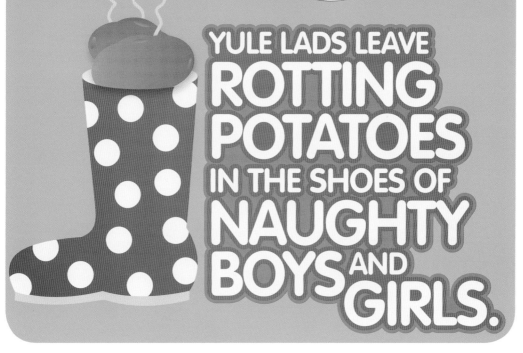

SPOON LICKER, SAUSAGE SWIPER, AND DOORWAY SNIFFER ARE THREE OF ICELAND'S 13 YULE LADS.

YULE LADS LEAVE ROTTING POTATOES IN THE SHOES OF NAUGHTY BOYS AND GIRLS.

117

A **525-pound** (238-kg) **block of cheese** was once delivered to the mayor of Garland, Texas, U.S.A., as **a Christmas gift.**

BEST PRESENT EVER!

IT TOOK SIX PEOPLE TO HAUL THE CHEESE TO THE MAYOR'S DOOR.

A man dressed as Santa Claus ran the 2015 Philadelphia Marathon in 2 hours 54 seconds.

Hundreds of runners hit the streets of Tokyo, Japan, in **Santa costumes** for the city's annual **Santa Claus Marathon.**

Three brothers in Minnesota, U.S.A., sculpted **A GIANT SEA TURTLE** made of snow that was nearly as tall as their house.

THE STAR ATOP THE CHRISTMAS TREE IN ROCKEFELLER CENTER IN NEW YORK CITY HAS

25,000
CRYSTALS
AND WEIGHS
550
POUNDS.
(249 kg)

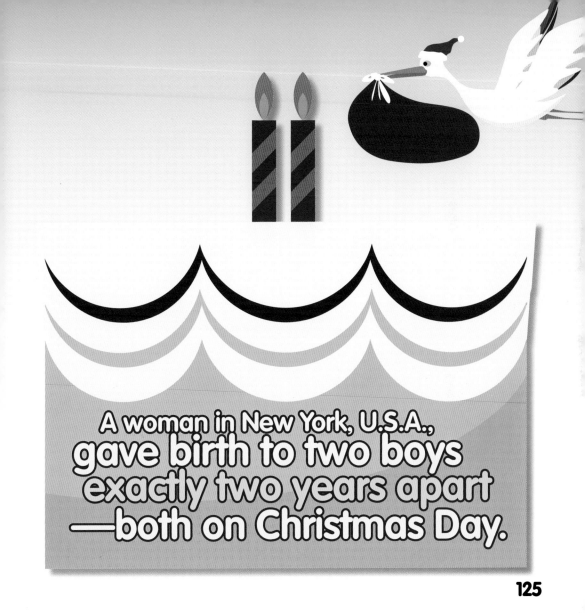

A woman in New York, U.S.A., gave birth to two boys exactly two years apart —both on Christmas Day.

IN HAWAII, U.S.A., **SANTA ARRIVES** ON AN OUTRIGGER **CANOE.**

In 2007, a group of **8,962** people simultaneously made **snow angels** in **North Dakota, U.S.A.**

Some people in **BOLIVIA** bring **ROOSTERS** to church on **CHRISTMAS EVE.**

EVERY CHRISTMAS YOU CAN WATCH A BURNING YULE LOG ON TV.

129

On Christmas Eve in Catalonia, Spain, children hit a hollow log called **TIÓ DE NADAL** with a stick until it "poops" out treats.

When there are no more treats, the log "poops" out garlic or onion.

The world's largest Advent calendar was nearly **233** feet *(71 m)* high and more than **75** feet *(23 m)* wide.

THE WORLD'S MOST EXPENSIVE ADVENT CALENDAR

CALENDAR

HELD 24 PRECIOUS DIAMONDS AND COST ALMOST

$2.7 MILLION.

A church in Germany turns its **24 FRONT WINDOWS** into a GIANT **ADVENT CALENDAR.**

Gengenbacher Adventskalender

Thomas Edison assembled the first strand of electric Christmas lights.

There are more than **600** species of Christmas trees in the world.

In some parts of Germany, SANTA leaves **GIFTS** in children's **SHOES.**

135

Santa has to cover **150 MILLION MILES** (241 million km) on his Christmas Eve journey, according to one scientist.

S M Tu W Th F

In parts of Belgium, Santa brings presents on

December 5

THE AMOUNT OF RIBBON USED TO WRAP GIFTS EACH CHRISTMAS IS ENOUGH TO TIE A BOW AROUND THE ENTIRE PLANET.

A pair of brothers had their picture taken on Santa's lap every year for more than 30 years straight.

You can BUY UPSIDE-DOWN ARTIFICIAL CHRISTMAS TREES to allow MORE GIFTS to be piled underneath.

December 25 is one of the least common birthdays.

AMERICANS SPEND AN AVERAGE OF THREE HOURS WRAPPING PRESENTS EVERY CHRISTMAS, ACCORDING TO ONE POLL.

ANCIENT ROMANS THOUGHT **HOLLY** PROTECTED AGAINST **LIGHTNING.**

Some Christmas lights can be seen from outer space.

Baltimore

Washington, D.C.

Richmond

Virginia Beach

...day Lighting

139

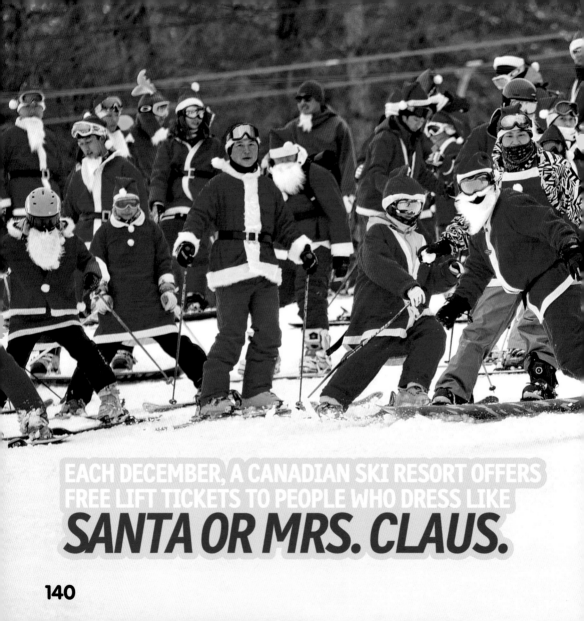

EACH DECEMBER, A CANADIAN SKI RESORT OFFERS
FREE LIFT TICKETS TO PEOPLE WHO DRESS LIKE
SANTA OR MRS. CLAUS.

A MAN SET A WORLD RECORD BY SLEDDING DOWN A SKI SLOPE AT **83.5 MILES** AN HOUR. (134 km/h)

141

Each Christmas, Spain hosts the world's largest lottery, with a jackpot of more than $2 billion.

You can buy
GINGERBREAD-SCENTED
DOG
SHAMPOO.

A 10-YEAR-OLD GIRL RECORDED THE HIT SONG
"I WANT A HIPPOPOTAMUS FOR CHRISTMAS."

SHE GOT ONE
(BUT DONATED IT TO A ZOO).

The ideal snow temperature for building a snowman? **30°F,** (-1.1°C) according to one engineer.

THAT'S WEIRD!

Hot chocolate was once considered a medicine.

In the United Kingdom, you can buy an **entire holiday dinner**—complete with layers of **egg, bacon, mince pies, sprouts,** and **Christmas pudding**— in **a can.**

Frankincense is sometimes used in toothpaste.

IN MEXICO, CHILDREN CELEBRATE CHRISTMAS BY BREAKING PIÑATAS.

Alabaster Snowball = the name of the elf in charge of

GREEK CHILDREN BELIEVE IN **GOBLINS** CALLED **KALLIKANTZAROI** THAT RUN **WILD** DURING THE 12 DAYS OF **CHRISTMAS.**

Santa's naughty-or-nice list, according to one tradition.

A NUTCRACKER MUSEUM **IN WASHINGTON STATE,**

U.S.A., HAS MORE THAN 6,000 NUTCRACKERS.

TO STOP THIEVES, OTHER PARKS HAVE **SPRAYED TREES** WITH **FOX URINE** AND A **CHEMICAL** THAT SMELLS LIKE **ROTTEN EGGS.**

THAT'S WEIRD!

In medieval Germany, people decorated their Christmas trees with apples, wafers, and cookies.

THE WORLD'S LARGEST **SECRET SANTA** EXCHANGE INVOLVED **1,463 STUDENTS** FROM KENTUCKY, U.S.A.

EARLY COOKIE CUTTERS WERE HANDMADE OUT OF TIN BY LOCAL "TINKERS"— OR TINSMITHS.

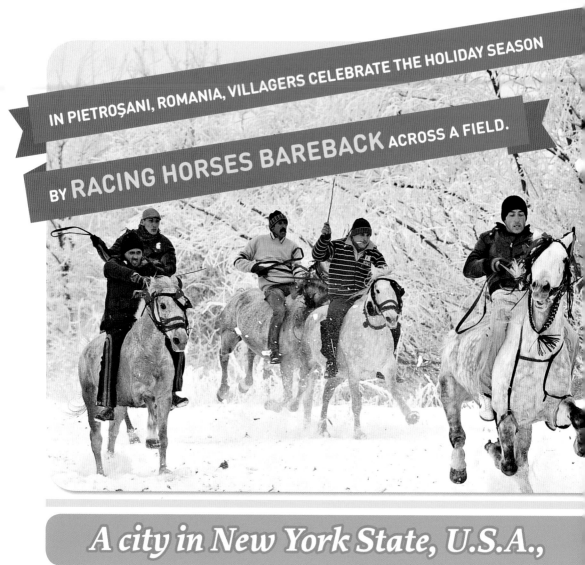

IN PIETROȘANI, ROMANIA, VILLAGERS CELEBRATE THE HOLIDAY SEASON BY RACING HORSES BAREBACK ACROSS A FIELD.

A city in New York State, U.S.A.,

once tried to outlaw snow.

REINDEER MIGRATE MORE THAN 600 MILES EVERY YEAR— (966 km) ABOUT THE DISTANCE FROM PARIS, FRANCE, TO BERLIN, GERMANY!

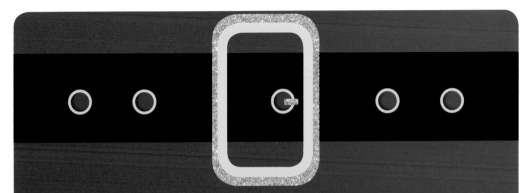

A SHOP IN HOLLYWOOD, CALIFORNIA, U.S.A., SELLS CUSTOM SANTA SUITS FOR UP TO **$2,500.**

It's a Christmas Eve tradition in Louisiana, U.S.A., to build bonfires on the Mississippi River levees.

Every December, the city of Oslo, Norway, sends the city of London, England, a **Christmas tree.**

U.S. PRESIDENT FRANKLIN DELANO ROOSEVELT RECEIVED A **110-POUND** FRUITCAKE (50-kg) AS A CHRISTMAS GIFT.

AN OREGON, U.S.A., CONGRESSMAN BAKES MORE THAN **200** FRUITCAKES EVERY CHRISTMAS.

ONE FAMILY PASSED DOWN THE SAME FRUITCAKE SINCE **1878.**

STUDIES SHOW THAT, ON AVERAGE, AMERICANS SPEND MORE THAN $800 ON CHRISTMAS PRESENTS EACH YEAR.

If you SPREAD OUT THE LIGHTS on the Christmas tree in ROCKEFELLER CENTER in New York City, they would STRETCH FOR FIVE MILES. (8 km)

Artificial SNOW can be made out of POTATO STARCH.

Best-selling Christmas toys have included ...

Battery-powered hamsters

A talking stuffed bear

A doll that wets herself

A glowing worm

A team in the Netherlands baked a sweet **CHRISTMAS BREAD** that was nearly **as LONG** as **A CITY BLOCK.**

Some women in medieval Europe ATE "GINGERBREAD HUSBANDS" to improve their chances of getting married.

MISTLETOE IS POISONOUS TO HUMANS.

The hook shape of a candy cane is believed to represent a shepherd's staff.

The **2.65 billion** *Christmas cards* sold each year in the United States could *fill a football field* **10** stories high.

IT TOOK **A MONTH** FOR RESIDENTS IN MAINE, U.S.A., TO BUILD A SNOWWOMAN AS TALL AS **A 12-STORY** BUILDING. IT HAD **SKIS** FOR EYELASHES AND **CAR TIRES** FOR LIPS.

164

A record-breaking **25,272** carolers gathered together in 2014 to sing Christmas songs in Nigeria, Africa.

MISTLETOE MOTHS lay their **EGGS** on and **FEED** on the popular holiday plant.

In the Middle Ages, *a Christmas meal in England* featured a **pig's head** and **mustard.**

WHITE HOUSE STAFF once hung **8,000 PAPER SNOWFLAKES** from the building's ceiling.

ONE **ASTROPHYSICIST** THINKS **SANTA** MAY USE **WORMHOLES** TO MAKE HIS YEARLY ROUNDS.

SANTA CLAUS CONQUERS THE *MARTIANS* IS A 1964 MOVIE ABOUT MARTIANS WHO COME TO EARTH TO KIDNAP SANTA.

169

A hundred years ago, candy and nuts were the most popular items on most kids' Christmas lists.

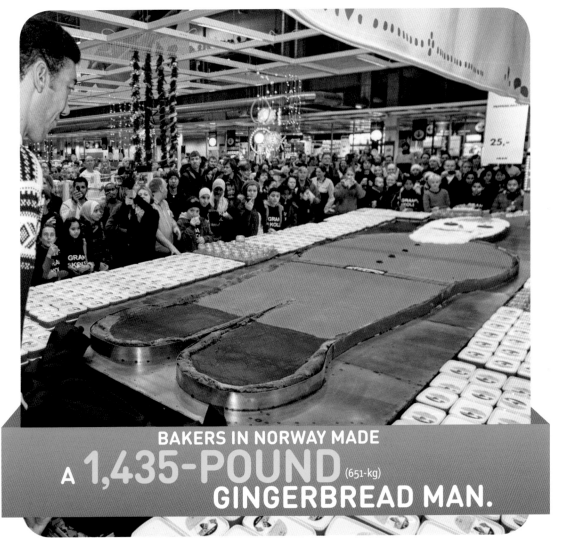

BAKERS IN NORWAY MADE
A **1,435-POUND** (651-kg)
GINGERBREAD MAN.

WHEN **WOOD FROGS** HIBERNATE, ABOUT **TWO-THIRDS** OF THEIR BODY'S **WATER** TURNS TO **ICE.**

Eating **peppermint candy** can trick your mouth into feeling cold, research says.

More than **62 PERCENT** of people "**RE-GIFT**" items to **FRIENDS** and **FAMILIES** each year, according to a survey.

IT'S TRADITION IN GERMANY FOR KIDS TO **LOOK** FOR AN **ORNAMENT** SHAPED LIKE A **PICKLE** HIDDEN ON THE TREE ON CHRISTMAS MORNING.

A MAN ONCE SENT CHRISTMAS CARDS TO **578** COMPLETE STRANGERS (AND 117 WROTE BACK!).

An estimated **8,200** people participated in a snowball fight in Saskatchewan, Canada.

In Greece, people **EXCHANGE** Christmas gifts on **JANUARY 1.**

Some people think **IT'S BAD LUCK** to take down a Christmas tree before **JANUARY 6.**

EGGNOG HAS BEEN AROUND SINCE THE 13TH CENTURY.

In Puerto Rico, eggnog is coconut flavored.

AT SOME ZOOS, ELEPHANTS MUNCH ON DISCARDED CHRISTMAS TREES AFTER THE HOLIDAYS.

People have been hanging stockings by fireplaces for more than 400 years.

The **candy cane** shrimp is named for its bright red-and-white striping.

In Guatemala, it's tradition for **JUST THE CHILDREN** to **OPEN PRESENTS ON CHRISTMAS.** (Parents and adults exchange gifts on New Year's Day.)

IN AUSTRALIA, SANTA CLAUS SOMETIMES ARRIVES BY HELICOPTER OR BOAT.

CHRISTMAS
BEETLES
SWARM
AUSTRALIA IN
THE
SUMMER.

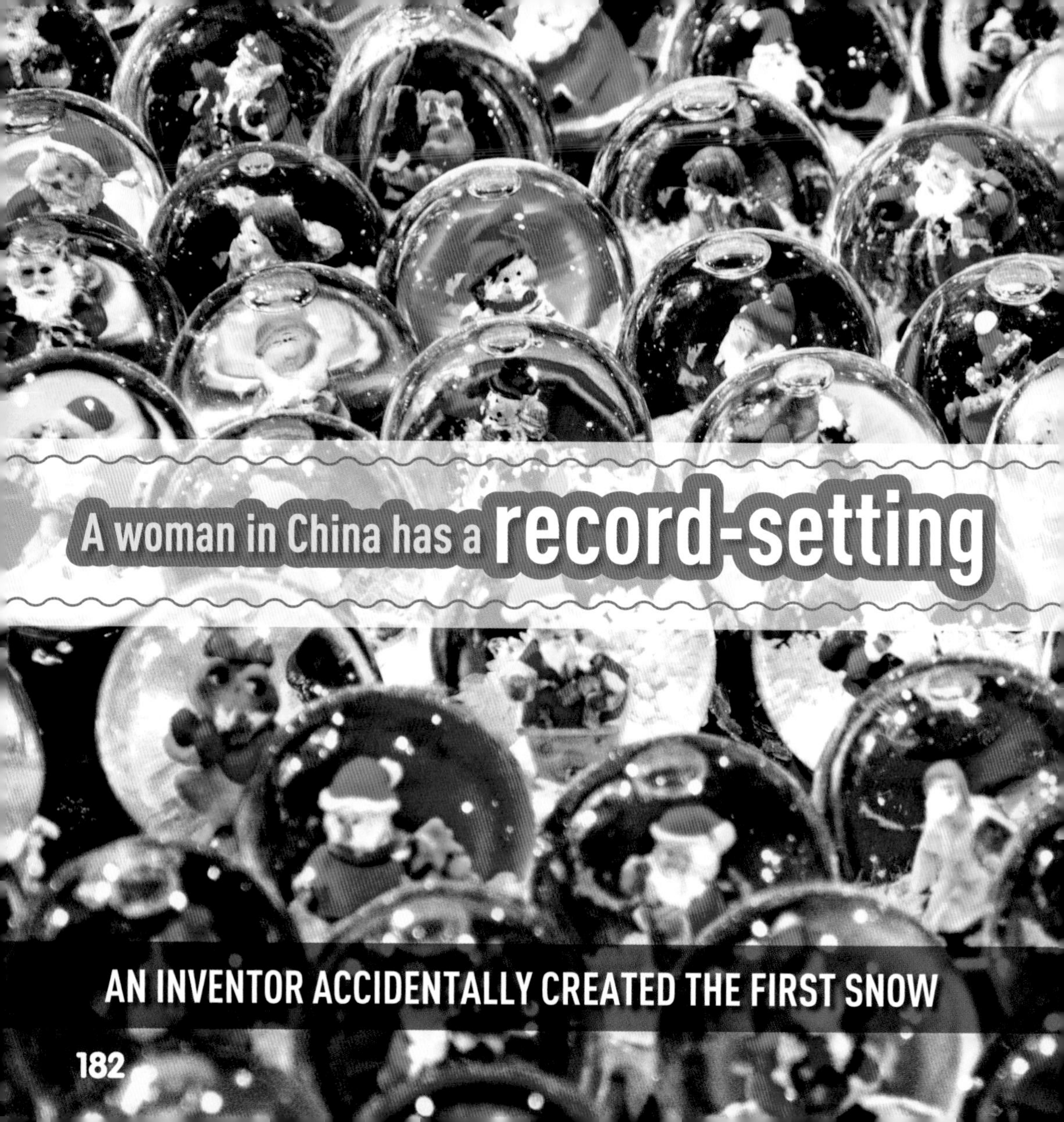

A woman in China has a **record-setting**

AN INVENTOR ACCIDENTALLY CREATED THE FIRST SNOW

collection of nearly **2,000** distinct snow globes.

GLOBE WHILE TRYING TO MAKE A LIGHTBULB BRIGHTER.

Jingle Bells was not originally written as a Christmas song.

The song's original title? "ONE-HORSE OPEN SLEIGH."

Mistletoe got its name from words meaning "dung on a twig."

A TEAM IN CANADA ONCE BUILT **2,069 SNOWMEN** IN ONE HOUR.

The Maya people boiled poinsettia roots to treat snakebites.

THAT'S WEIRD!

IF **SANTA** TRAVELED AT THE **SPEED OF LIGHT,** HE COULD **CIRCLE THE GLOBE SEVEN TIMES IN ONE SECOND.**

187

A MAN DRESSED AS SANTA CLAUS WENT SKYDIVING OVER THE NORTH POLE.

HO HO HO!

Oranges *were once* popular stocking stuffers.

ABOUT **10** MILLION TURKEYS ARE CONSUMED IN THE UNITED KINGDOM AT CHRISTMAS.

DURING THE U.S. CIVIL WAR, CONFEDERATE TROOPS HAD A 9,000-PERSON SNOWBALL FIGHT.

YULE DOO =
A CHRISTMAS
ORNAMENT
THAT LOOKS LIKE
GLITTERING
DOG POO

193

In the 1800s, Pennsylvania Dutch children hung decorated Christmas cookies in the windows of their homes.

People used to **dye popcorn** **bright** **colors** to string on THEIR CHRISTMAS TREES.

IN 1836, ALABAMA WAS THE FIRST U.S. STATE TO RECOGNIZE CHRISTMAS AS AN OFFICIAL HOLIDAY.

IN **1907**, OKLAHOMA WAS THE LAST U.S. STATE TO RECOGNIZE CHRISTMAS AS AN OFFICIAL HOLIDAY.

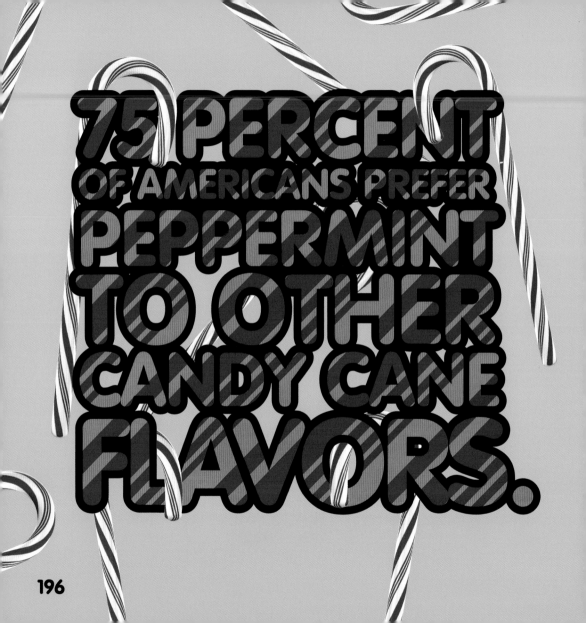

75 PERCENT OF AMERICANS PREFER PEPPERMINT TO OTHER CANDY CANE FLAVORS.

CANADA HAS A SPECIAL POST OFFICE FOR LETTERS TO SANTA.

ITS POSTAL CODE IS HoH oHo.

IT'S TRADITION IN SWEDEN TO WATCH DONALD DUCK CARTOONS ON CHRISTMAS EVE.

THE MYTHICAL KRAMPUS IS SAID TO SWAT NAUGHTY CHILDREN ON CHRISTMAS.

It would cost you more than

$34,000

to buy all the gifts in the song
"THE TWELVE DAYS OF CHRISTMAS."

A species of snail is named Ba humbugi.

Families in central Europe traditonally store carp in their bathtubs for a few days before preparing them for Christmas dinner.

It's tradition in Peru to drink hot chocolate with Christmas breakfast.

FACTFINDER

Boldface indicates illustrations.

FACTFINDER

FACTFINDER

Since 1888, the National Geographic Society has funded more than 12,000 research, exploration, and preservation projects around the world. The Society receives funds from National Geographic Partners, LLC, funded in part by your purchase. A portion of the proceeds from this book supports this vital work. To learn more, visit natgeo.com/info.

For more information, visit nationalgeographic.com, call 1-877-873-6846, or write to the following address:

National Geographic Partners
1145 17th Street N.W.
Washington, D.C. 20036-4688 U.S.A.

Visit us online at nationalgeographic.com/books

For librarians and teachers:
nationalgeographic.com/books/librarians-and-educators

More for kids from National Geographic:
natgeokids.com

For rights or permissions inquiries, please contact National Geographic Books Subsidiary Rights: bookrights@natgeo.com

Designed by Julide Dengel

Title: Weird but true Christmas / by National Geographic Kids.
Other titles: National Geographic kids.
Description: Washington, DC : National Geographic Kids, [2017] | Series: Weird but true | Includes index. | Audience: Ages: 8-12. | Audience: Grades: 4 to 6.
Identifiers: LCCN 2017010392| ISBN 9781426328893 (paperback : alk. paper) | ISBN 9781426328909 (hardcover)
Subjects: LCSH: Christmas--Juvenile literature.
Classification: LCC GT4985.5 .W47 2017 | DDC 263/.915--dc23
LC record available at https://lccn.loc.gov/2017010392

The publisher would like to thank Avery Hurt, author and researcher; Sarah Wassner Flynn, author and researcher; Jen Agresta, project manager; Paige Towler, project editor; Hillary Leo of Royal Scruff, photo editor; Lori Epstein, photo director; Alix Inchausti, production editor; and Anne LeongSon, design production assistant.

Printed in Hong Kong
20/PPHK/4

PHOTO CREDITS

30 WONDERFUL WAYS TO SAY THANKS!

Friends! Family! Teachers! Neighbors! There are plenty of awesome people to thank and reasons to be thankful throughout the year, and this book can help you do so.

FIND INSIDE!
30 PULL-OUT THANK-YOU CARDS featuring adorable animals and funny sayings!